a.vase

Alison Gibb

NEWTON-LE-WILLOWS

Published in the United Kingdom in 2017
by The Knives Forks And Spoons Press,
51 Pipit Avenue,
Newton-le-Willows,
Merseyside,
WA12 9RG.

ISBN 978-1-909443-94-5

Copyright © Alison Gibb, 2017.

The right of Alison Gibb to be identified as the author of this work has been asserted by her in accordance with the Copyrights, Designs and Patents Act of 1988. All rights reserved. No part of this publication may be reproduced, stored in a retrieval system, transmitted in any form or by any means, electronic, photocopying, recording or otherwise, without prior permission of the publisher.

Acknowledgements:

Many thanks to: Robert Hampson, Kristen Kreider at Royal Holloway, University of London and to James Davies, Tom Jenks and Scott Thurston for inviting me to perform this work at The Other Room reading series in Manchester, and for featuring work from this project in The Other Room Anthology 7, 2015.

Table of Contents

a.vase   13

a. vase fragments   27

A NOTE ON THE TEXT

This pamphlet brings together poetry and drawings I developed in response to museum restorations methods, as strategies for creating and performing experimental poetry texts and images.

a.vase

a.vase restoration (1 of 5)

Fragments of a vessel which are to be glued together must match one another in the smallest details, although they need not be like one another. In the same way a translation, instead of resembling the meaning of the original, must lovingly and in detail incorporate the original's mode of signification thus making both the original and the translation recognizable as fragments of a greater language, just as fragments are part of a vessel.

Walter Benjamin, from *The Task of the Translator*, (1999)

a.vase

a.vase

A vase
A. vase blue & white

White

A vase (/'vɑːz/, /'veɪs/, or

/'veɪz/)

Is an opening /a. container

Often used to hold cut flowers

Alison Gibb

There. Were no flowers in the a.vase I
Placed on my desk. Blue. I smashed a.vase
Into a varity of shapes & sizes. a. vase.
P a i n t e d. A white pottery vase. D e c o
R a t e d under the g l a z e with cobalt oxide.
Traces of gilding. *Clay*. Kaolin & Kiln.

a.vase

A. vase. *Blue.* O n w h i t e
Porcelain. Pieces so small
They are. Blue. Exploded into s m i t h e
R e e n s . A vase is often decorated to
Extend the beauty of its contents.
& are defined as having a certain
Anatomy. Cool & smooth. Porcelain.
I held it in my hands.

Two vases s h a t t e r e d into
Hundreds of pieces while the third
Broke into a few
Chinese b l u e & White w a r e s
Incorporated into Islamic Designs.
Mullite & Cobalt oxide.
A. vase has a certain anatomy.

a.vase

/Pieces so small they are
/White.

Pieces so small they are
 /Like dust. /

Pieces so small they / are
of similar /size.

Alison Gibb

A vase has a foot & a distinguishable base.
The design of the *base* may be bulbous. Flat.
C a r i n a t e or another s h a p e . The design *of*
The base *of* a. vase is. Flat. It is not bulbous.
It is not carinate. It is n o t o r another *shape.*

a.vase

Next. The body. Which forms the main &
Largest portion of the piece. Blue. With a raised
Lip. To run your finger around. Song blue-&-white.
Graphite. Soot & animal glue. Next.

Alison Gibb

Next. a. vase has a body. Which forms the main & Largest portion of the piece. White. Decorated. With a Raised *lip. Decorated with flowers.* Is a. v a s e.

a.vase

Resting atop the body is the shoulder.
Where the body curves inward.
D e c o r a t e d with blossoms in blue.
Around a. vase. I kept it on my desk
Paper. Iron & ink.

Alison Gibb

Then. The neck. Where the vase is given
More height. A third of the way down
A border in blue. A crisscross pattern with
Inlays of the blossom pattern wrap around
A.vase. a. vase has no neck. Just shoulders
Between the body & the l i p. I h e l d a. vase
In my hand. History mix e d w i t h t t a n n in
& thickened.

a.vase

Lastly. The lip. Where a vase
Flares out at the top. Clay. Kaolin
& Kiln. A. vase. Is curved. With
A flat base & a hole for flowers
Smaller. At the t o p
With a pear shaped
Drop. Lip *raised*. V i s i b l e.

a.vase *fragments*

a.vase

Alison Gibb

a.vase

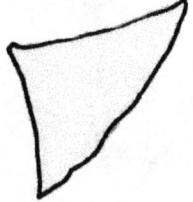

Alison Gibb

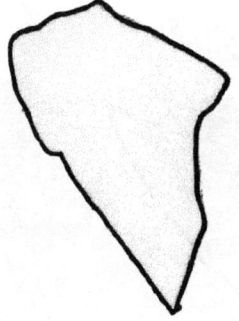

a.vase

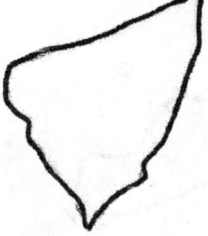

Alison Gibb

a.vase

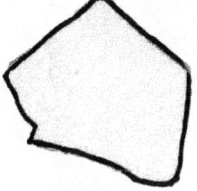

Alison Gibb

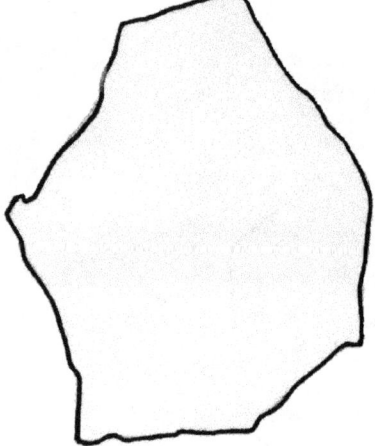

a.vase

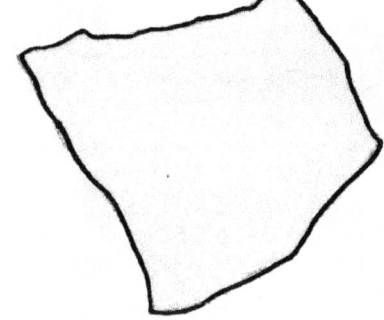

Alison Gibb

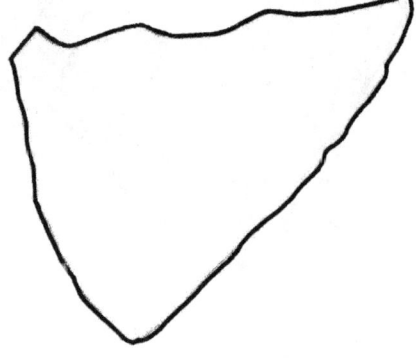

a.vase

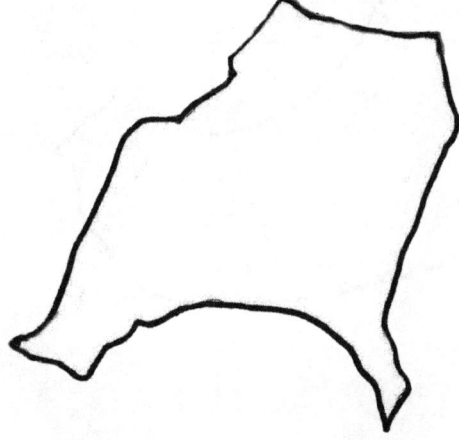

Alison Gibb

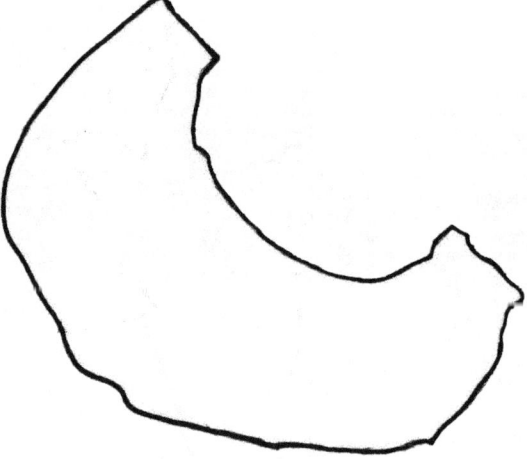

a.vase

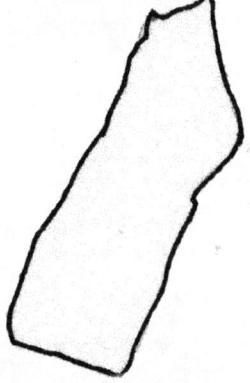

Alison Gibb

a.vase

Alison Gibb

a.vase

Alison Gibb

a.vase

Alison Gibb

a.vase

Alison Gibb

a.vase

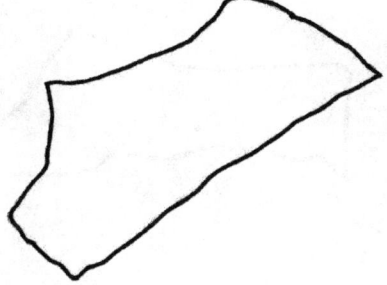

Alison Gibb

a.vase

Alison Gibb

a.vase

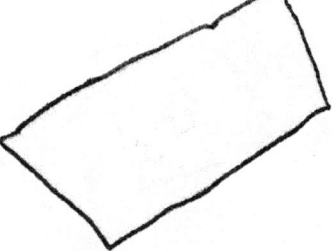

Alison Gibb
_____

a.vase

Alison Gibb

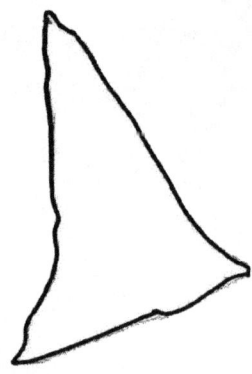

a.vase
_____

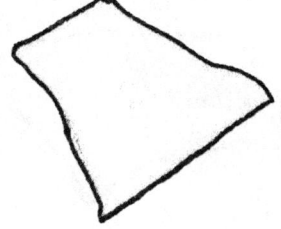

Alison Gibb

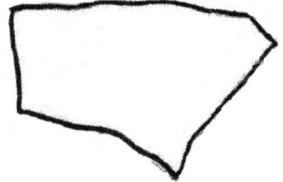

a.vase

Alison Gibb

a.vase

Alison Gibb

a.vase

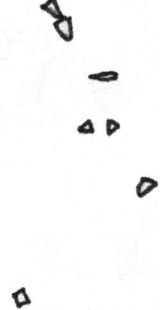

Alison Gibb

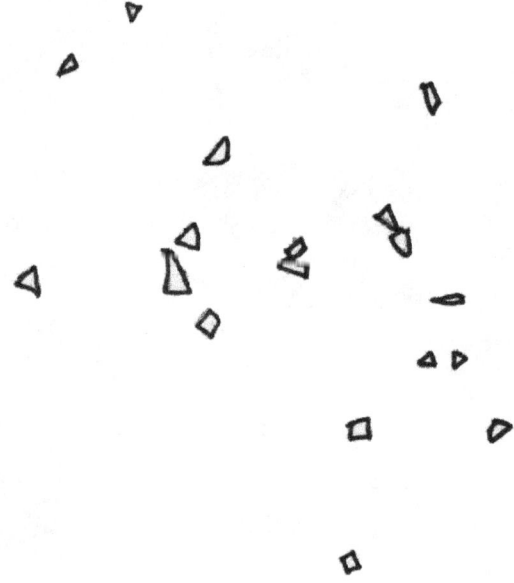

a.vase

Alison Gibb

a.vase

Alison Gibb

www.ingramcontent.com/pod-product-compliance
Lightning Source LLC
Chambersburg PA
CBHW051702040426
42446CB00009B/1268